Bruce McMillan

GHOST DOLL

HOUGHTON MIFFLIN COMPANY BOSTON 1983

For Chrissy

Library of Congress Cataloging in Publication Data

McMillan, Bruce.
  Ghost doll.

  Summary: Chrissy overcomes her fear of ghosts
to help a long-forgotten doll. Illustrated with photo-
graphs taken in a house built in 1812 and listed in the
National Register of Historic Places.
  [1. Ghosts — Fiction. 2. Dolls — Fiction] I. Title.
PZ7.M47878Gh   1983   [E]   83-8386
ISBN 0-395-33073-4

Printed in the United States of America

Y 10 9 8 7 6 5 4 3 2 1

The house on the hill was haunted, some people said,
but nobody ever told Chrissy.

She heard a call from inside the house. A faint voice cried,
"Come in. Come in. Come in and play with me."

It was hard to see through the thin white curtain, and what she saw
wasn't very clear. It looked like a doll, yet it didn't. And it seemed to glow
in the old house.

Chrissy opened the creaky front door and peered inside.
She didn't hear the voice now. Everything was very quiet.

What she had seen wasn't there anymore.
She looked everywhere, but it was gone.

Then, from the next room, something called again.
"I'm in here. I'm in here. Please come in here."

Chrissy followed the voice, but she still couldn't see what was calling her.
It stayed hidden in the ceiling shadows.

Had she really heard something? Chrissy sat down to think. She was wondering if she had imagined it all when down from the ceiling floated . . .

. . . a ghostly figure. Chrissy was so surprised she shrieked, "Aaaahhhh!"
But she wasn't the only one to be surprised.

The frightened ghost flew off in a flash.
Chrissy thought she had better leave this strange old house.

She was hurrying back the way she had come when she heard a whisper.
"Please don't go." Chrissy glanced up the stairs.

The soft voice calmed Chrissy's fears. "I'm lonely.
I don't want to live here by myself and be a ghost forever."
The ghost doll floated down toward Chrissy.

"I wasn't always a ghost. A long time ago, I was a real doll.
A little girl brought me into this house to play, but something
frightened her. She went away and forgot me. She never came back."

"I've been here so long I've become a ghost. I could be a doll again —
your doll, if you really want me." Before Chrissy could answer,
the ghost doll turned and floated up the stairs.

As it drifted out of sight, it called back softly, "I'll be your doll
if you show me you're brave. I don't want to be left alone ever again."

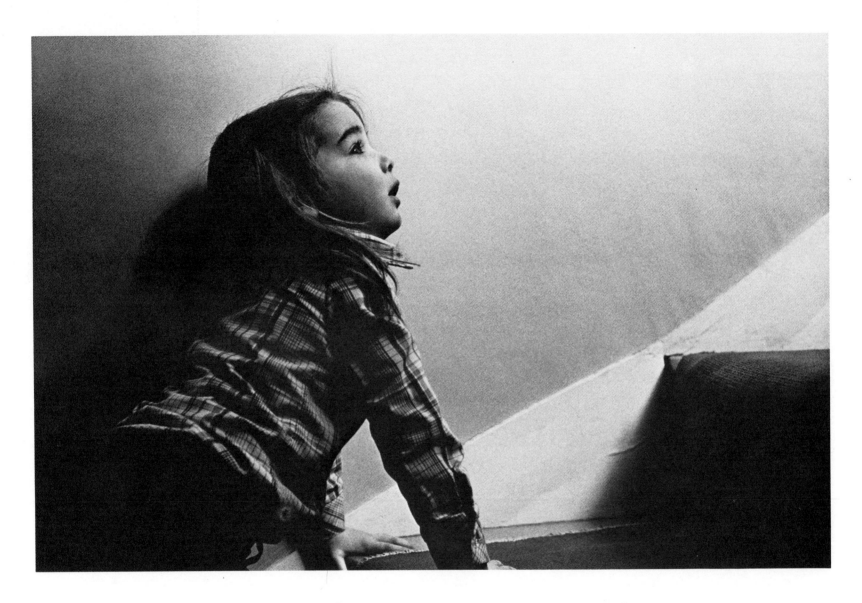

Chrissy climbed the stairs, looking for the ghost doll. She hesitated at each step until, finally, she found herself at the very top of the house.

She watched and waited. Then, even though she didn't see it, she heard the ghost doll speak. "Touch me!"

At first Chrissy didn't move. But when the ghost doll reached out,
Chrissy reached out, too, and they touched.

"You didn't run away! You wouldn't leave me.
Now I'm sure! I want to be your doll."

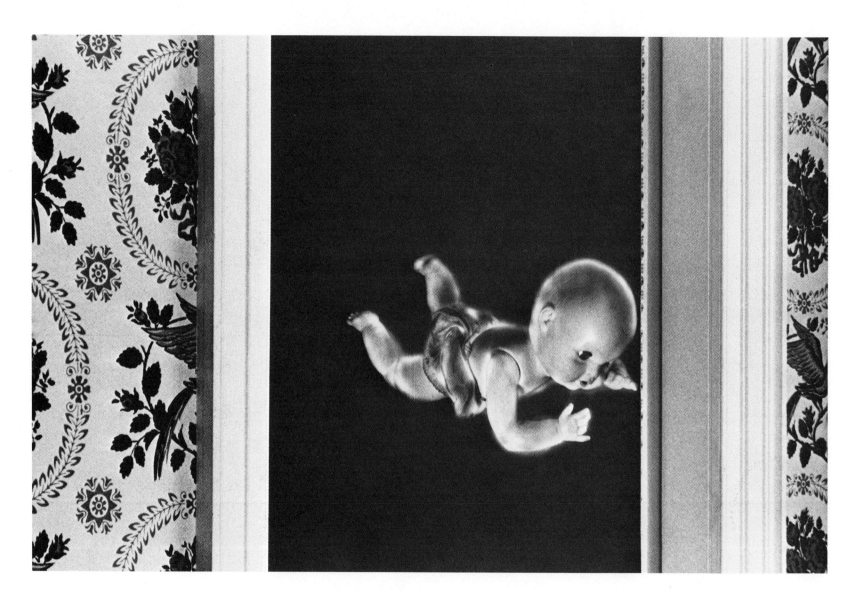

But suddenly, before Chrissy knew what was happening, the ghost doll
flew back down the stairs. Although Chrissy ran as fast as she could,
she couldn't keep up.

It floated into a box, where it began to lose its eerie glow.

Chrissy caught up to it in time to see the almost invisible form fading away.

She was about to go closer when, without warning, the box lid flew on.
Chrissy gasped.

She didn't know what to do. Should she open the box?
Should she look inside? Chrissy didn't have to decide.

The box flew right past her, through another room, back into the hall,
and on down the stairs.

It didn't stop in the downstairs hall but went straight out the front door, which Chrissy had forgotten to shut. She chased after it, afraid she would never see the ghost doll again.

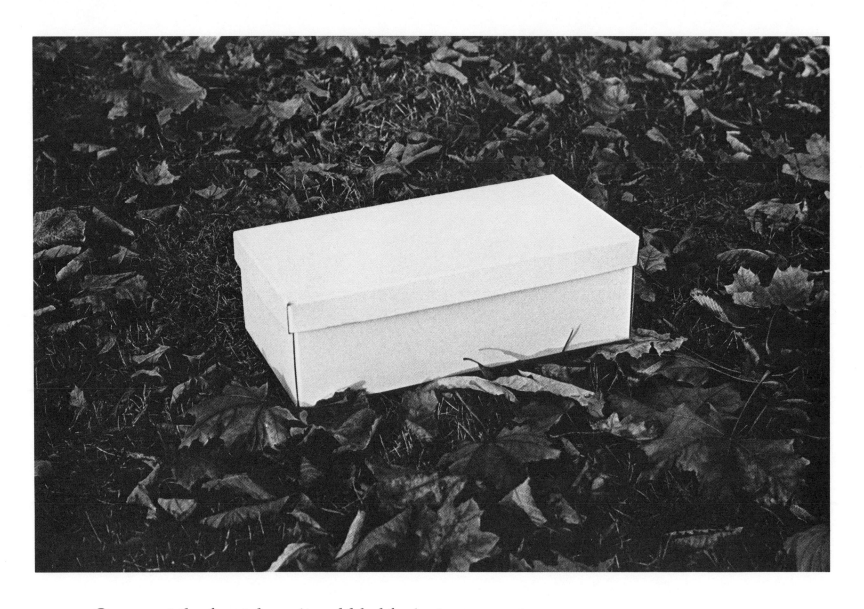

Once past the front door, it wobbled for just a moment.

Then, in a gliding fall, it came to rest on the leaf-covered grass.

What was inside? A ghost? A doll? Anything at all?
Chrissy didn't know. She looked back at the house,
then at the box and, holding her breath, lifted the lid.

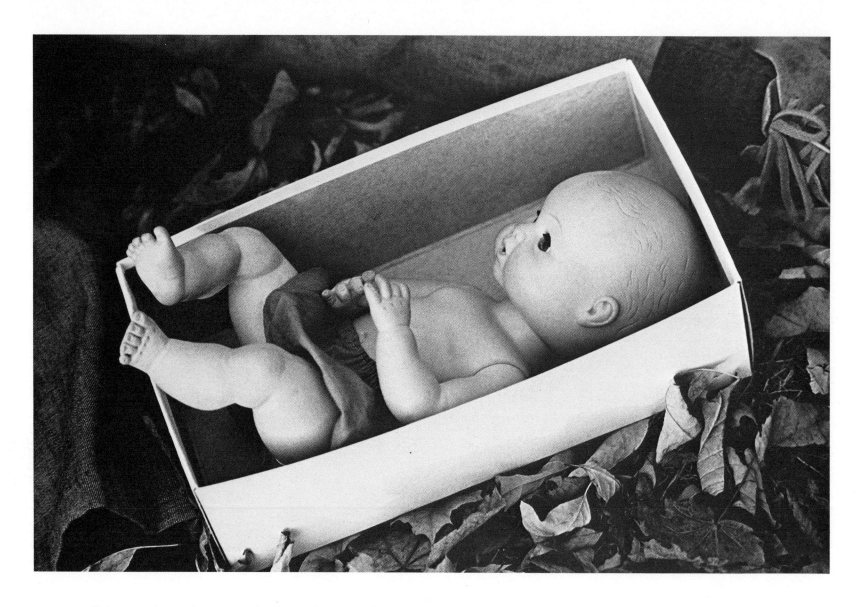

It wasn't a ghost. It didn't glow. It didn't speak.
It was a doll, a real doll, that Chrissy picked up and hugged . . .

. . . a doll that would never be left alone again.

Thanks to:
Chrissy Wallingford for pretending so well, and her mother, Rachel, for all her coaching and help; Rick Littlefield and Bev Davis, innkeepers and owners of the Captain Lord Mansion Guest House in Kennebunkport, Maine, for the unlimited use of the mansion, where the book was entirely photographed, and which, incidentally, was built in 1812 and is listed in the National Register of Historic Places; Marlene Parent and her daughters, Karen and Sarah, for providing the doll; Lois Lazaroff for the doll's outfit; and everyone at the Springvale Public Library and The Upper Story Bookstore, both in Springvale, Maine, for providing the many dolls from which to choose.